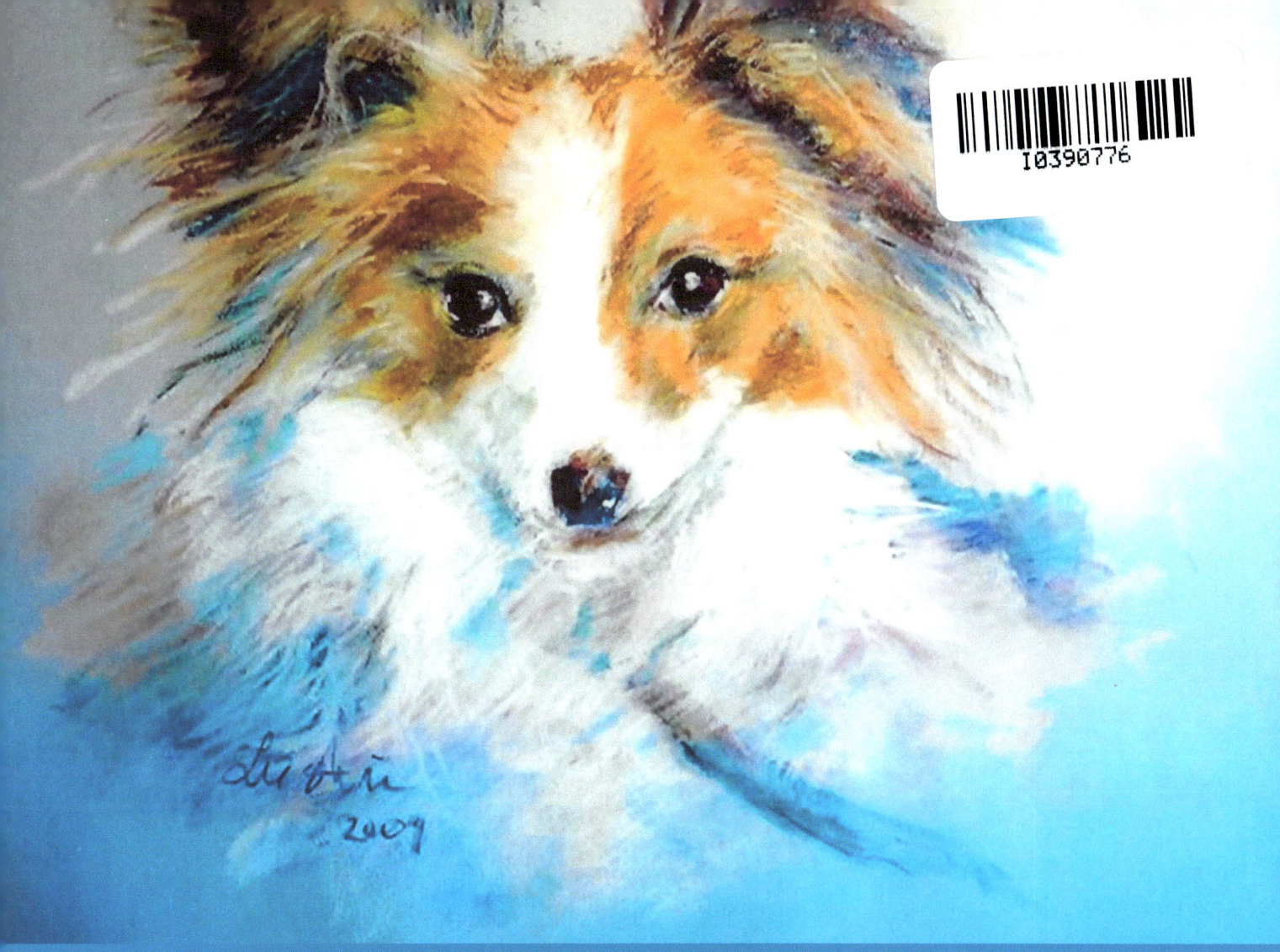

Art by Sulastri With Quotes

Written by Rich Linville
ISBN: 9781087090535

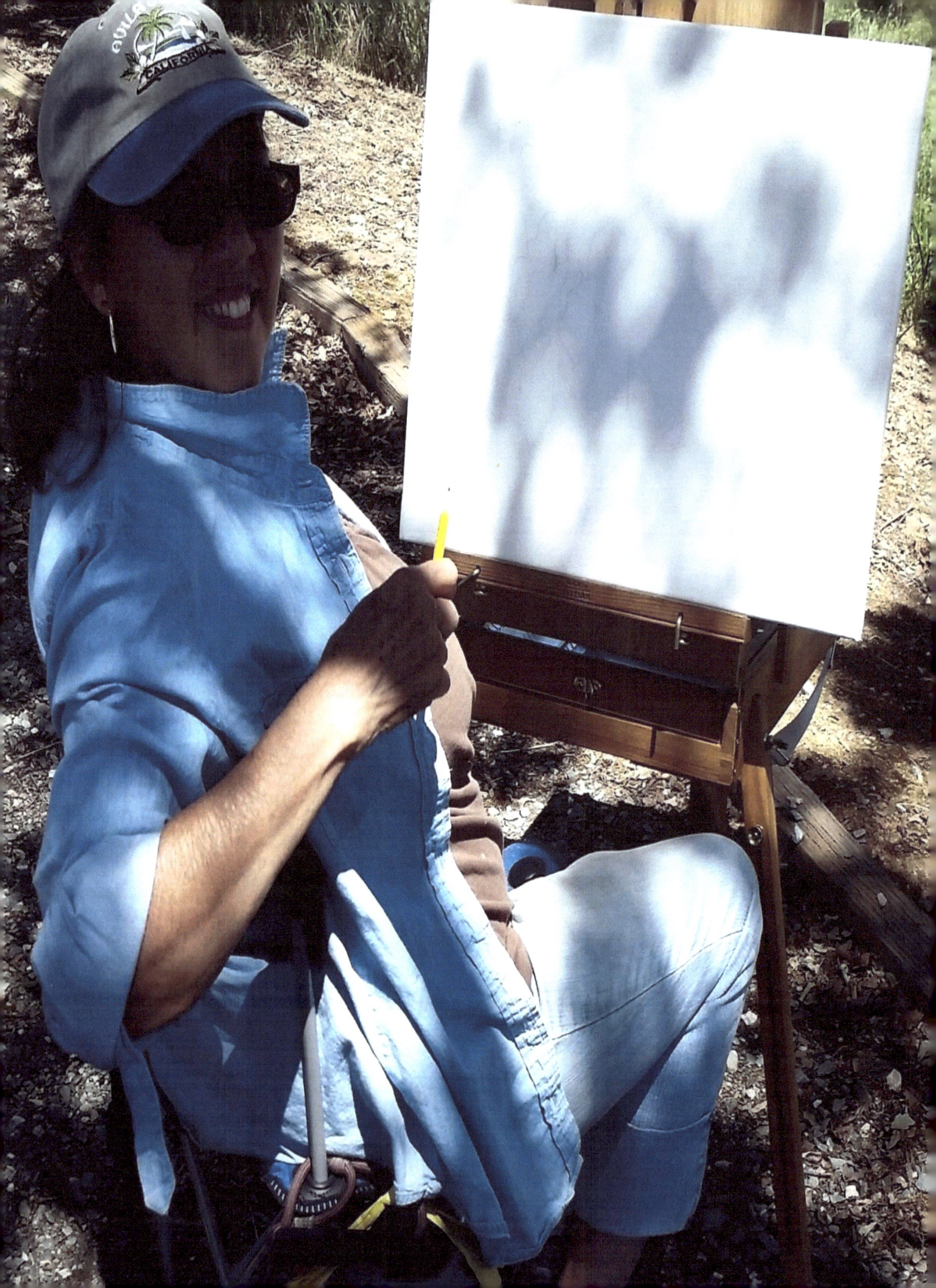

Born in Holland and studying in Jakarta, Indonesia, Sulastri has been doing art since she was young. After moving to the United States she attended art classes at a community college and advanced herself at a private Art Academy in Sonora, California. She has done watercolors, pen and inks, oils, charcoals, and pastels. Her subjects include scenery, people, pets, and other animals. Her paintings show a deep love of life and nature. Living in the beautiful Sierra Nevada Mountains, Sulastri shares her unique impressions of the world. For information about her original art, prints, and commissions, contact the artist at (209) 918-2534.

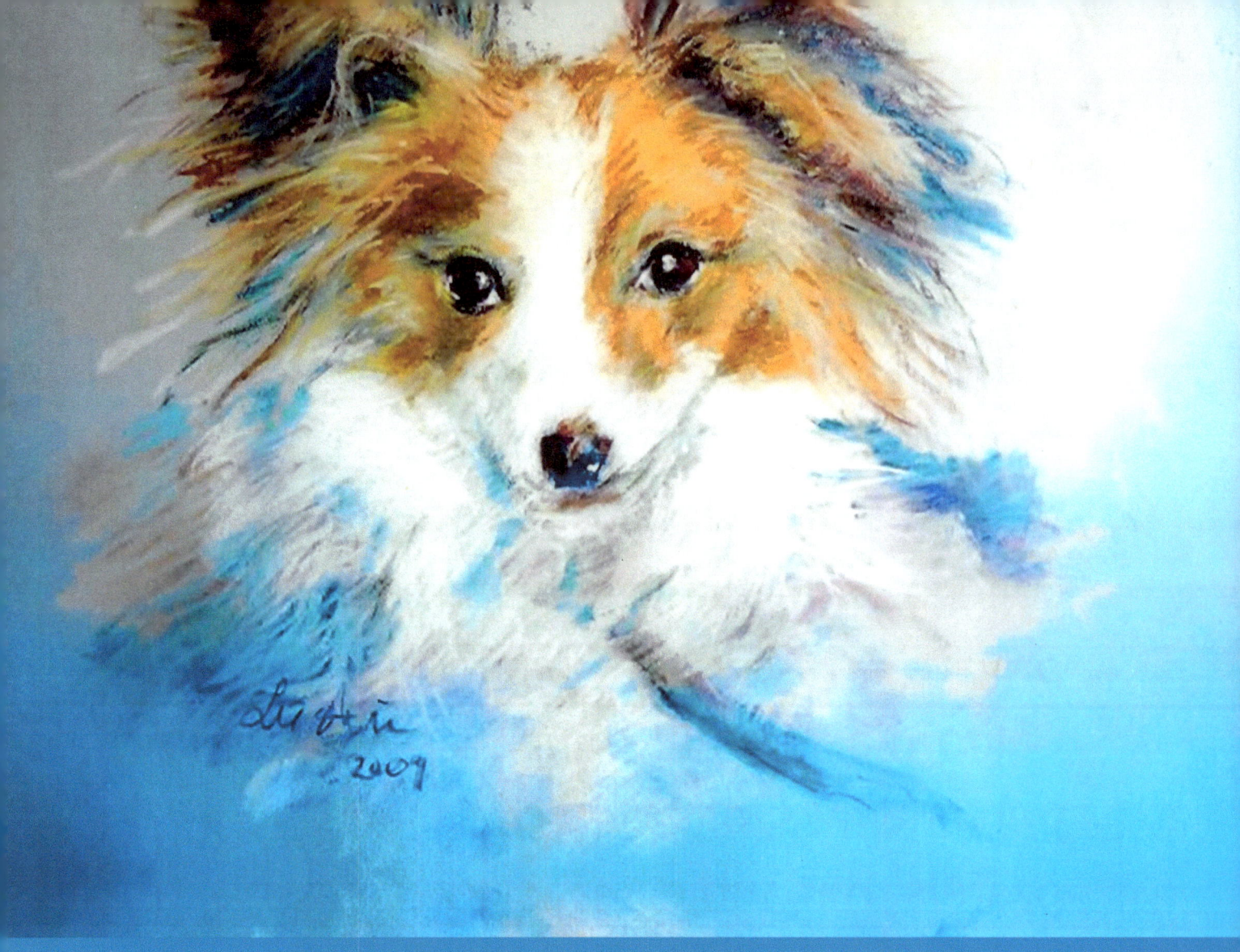

"As a matter of fact, the world does revolve around my Papillon Dog!"
- Anonymous

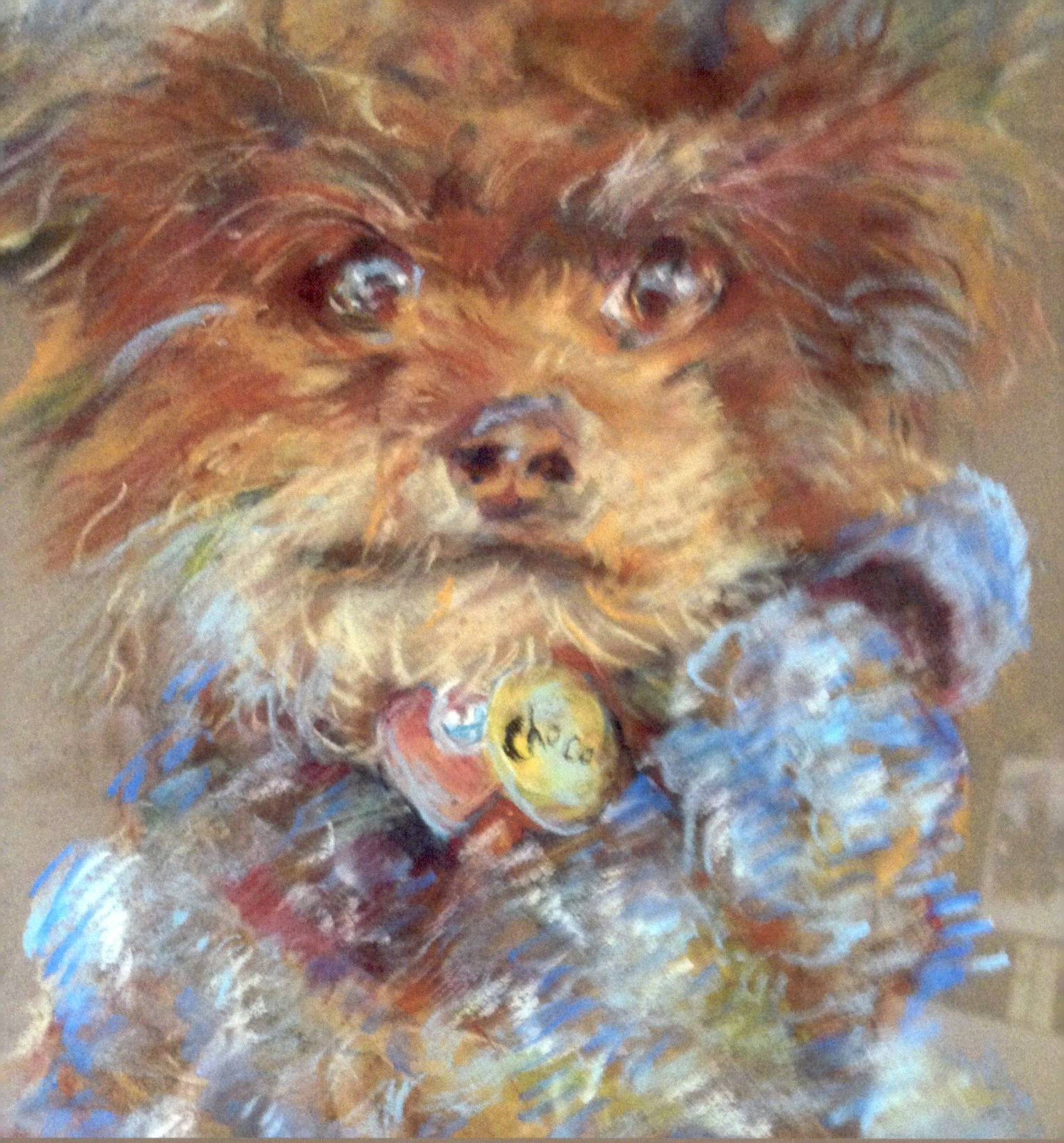

"I'm called a Chick Magnet. I am part chihuahua and part toy poodle and part gremlin!" - Anonymous

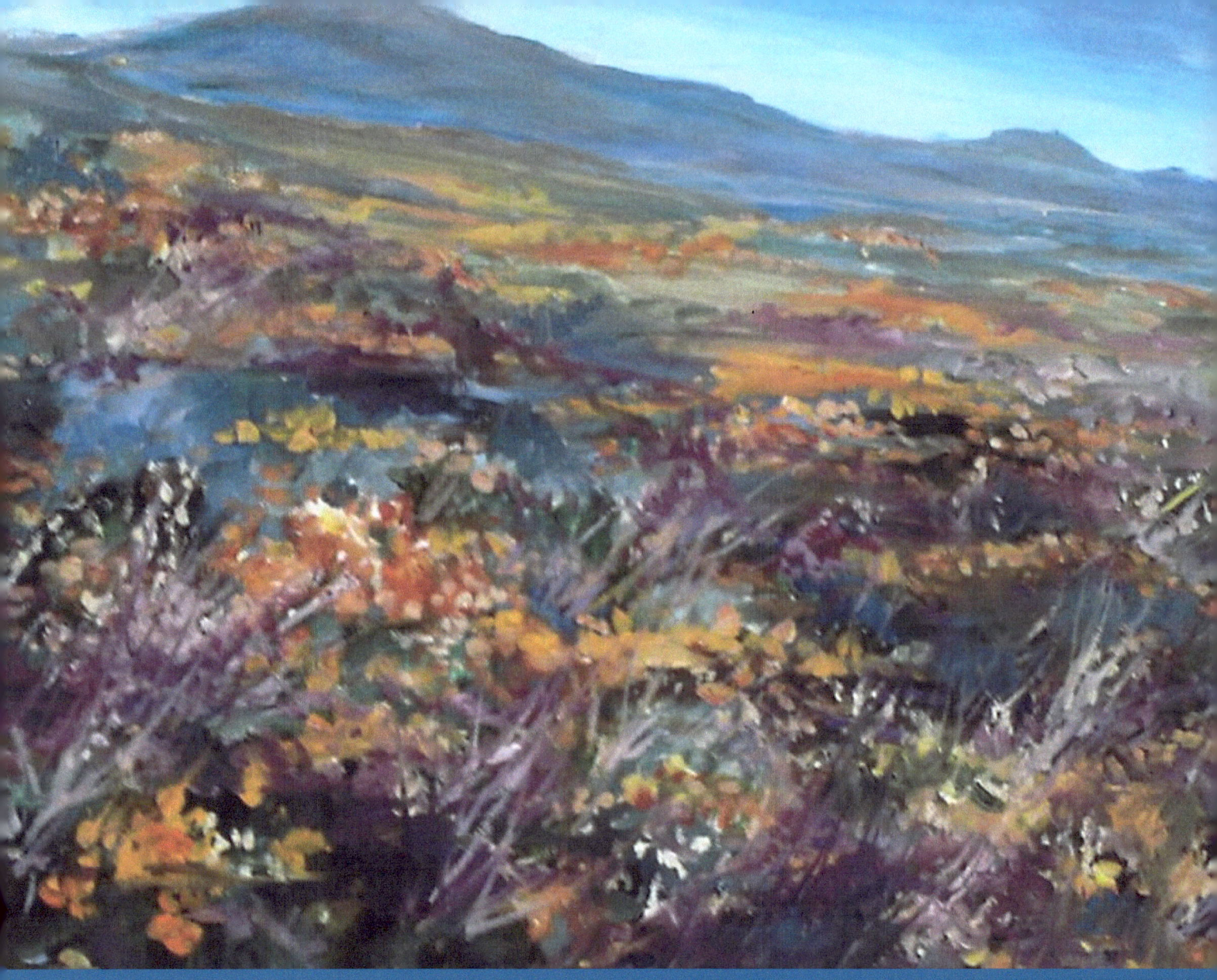

"Mother Nature has the best box of crayons!"
- Anonymous

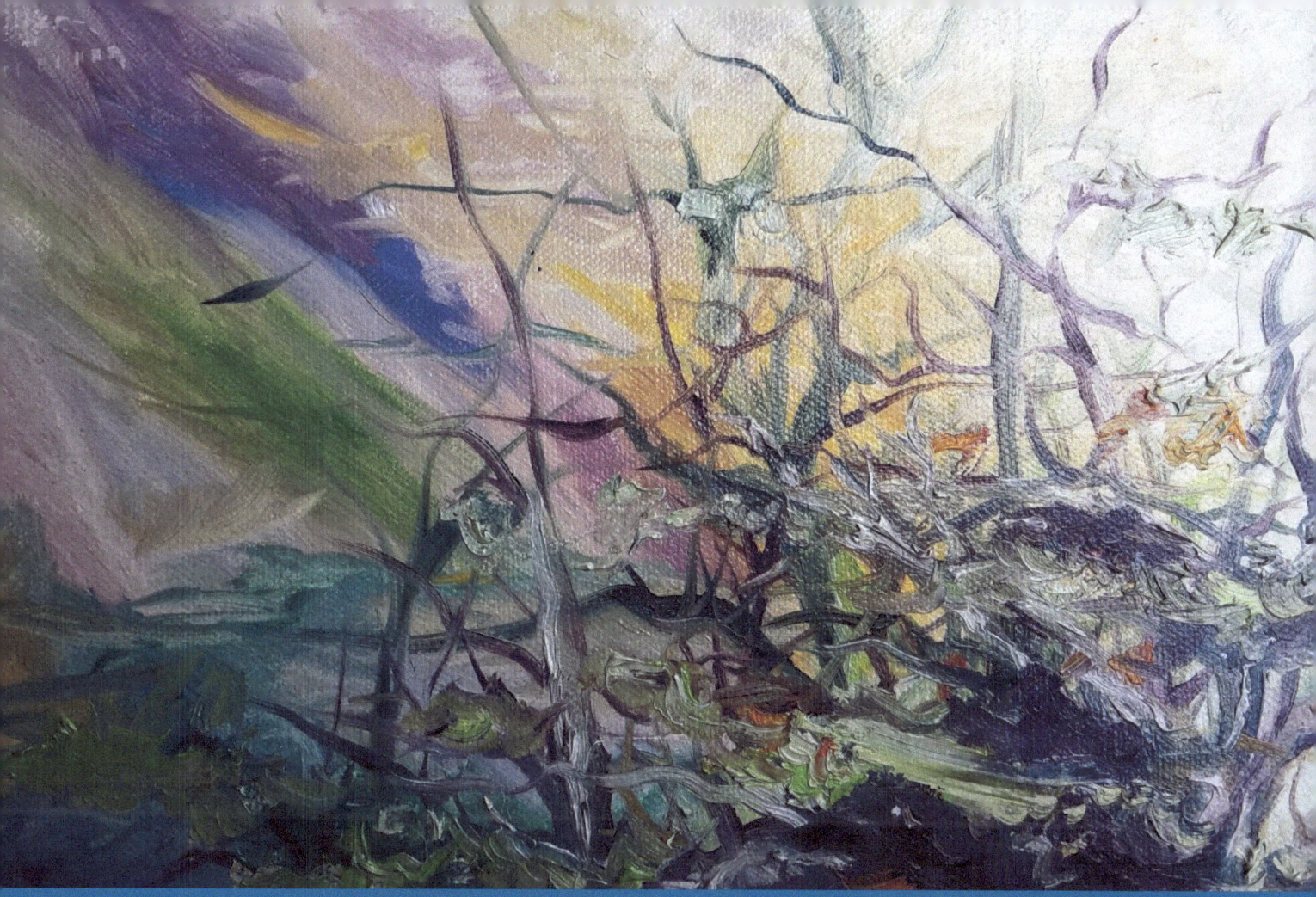

"What are the thorns really telling her? It's why she won't let us see them, why she clings to them--or they cling to her--as though she got herself buried in a bramble thicket and she can't get out and we can't get in to free her." - Patricia A. McKillip, Alphabet of Thorn

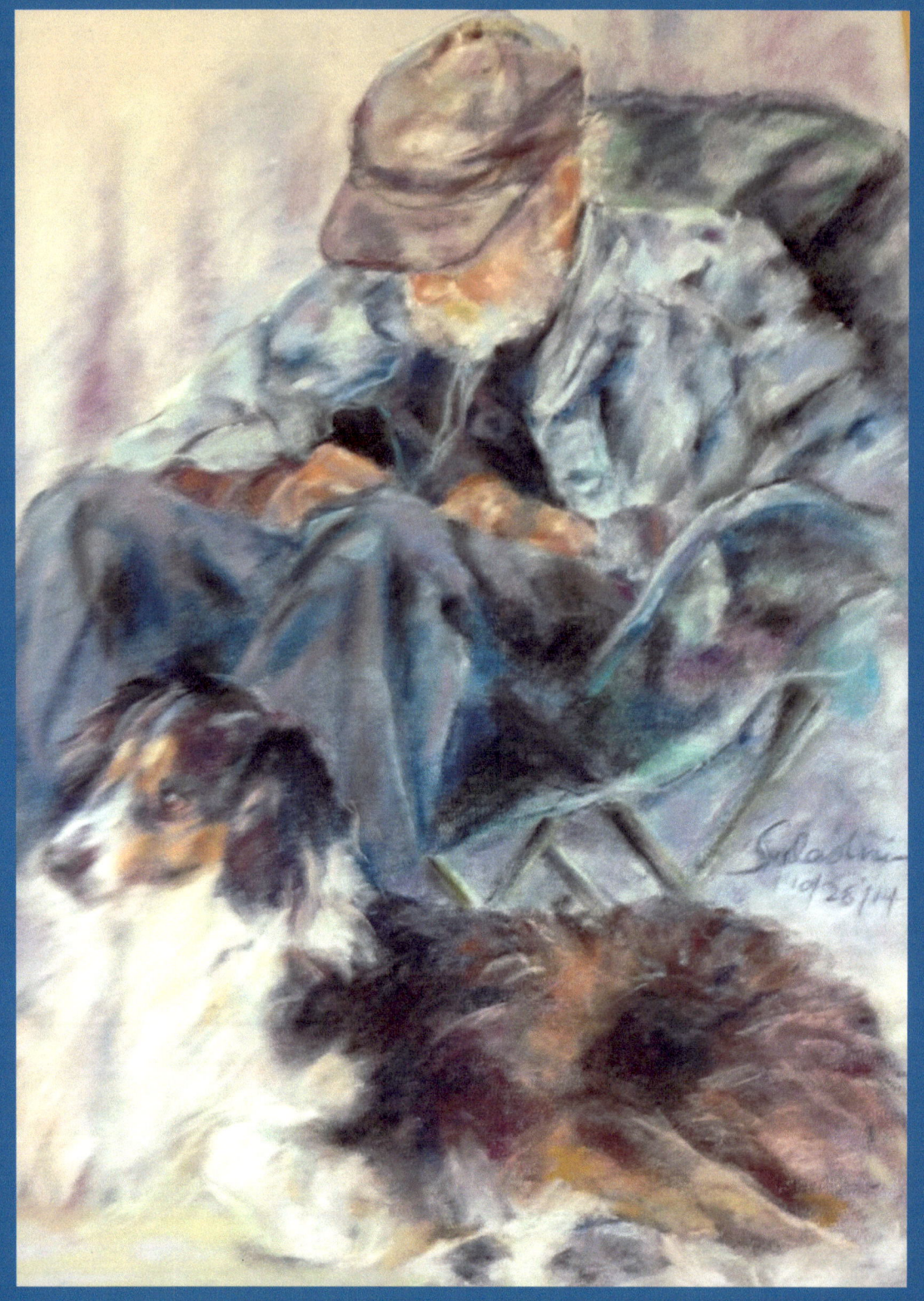

"The key to retirement is to find joy in the little things."
- Susan Miller

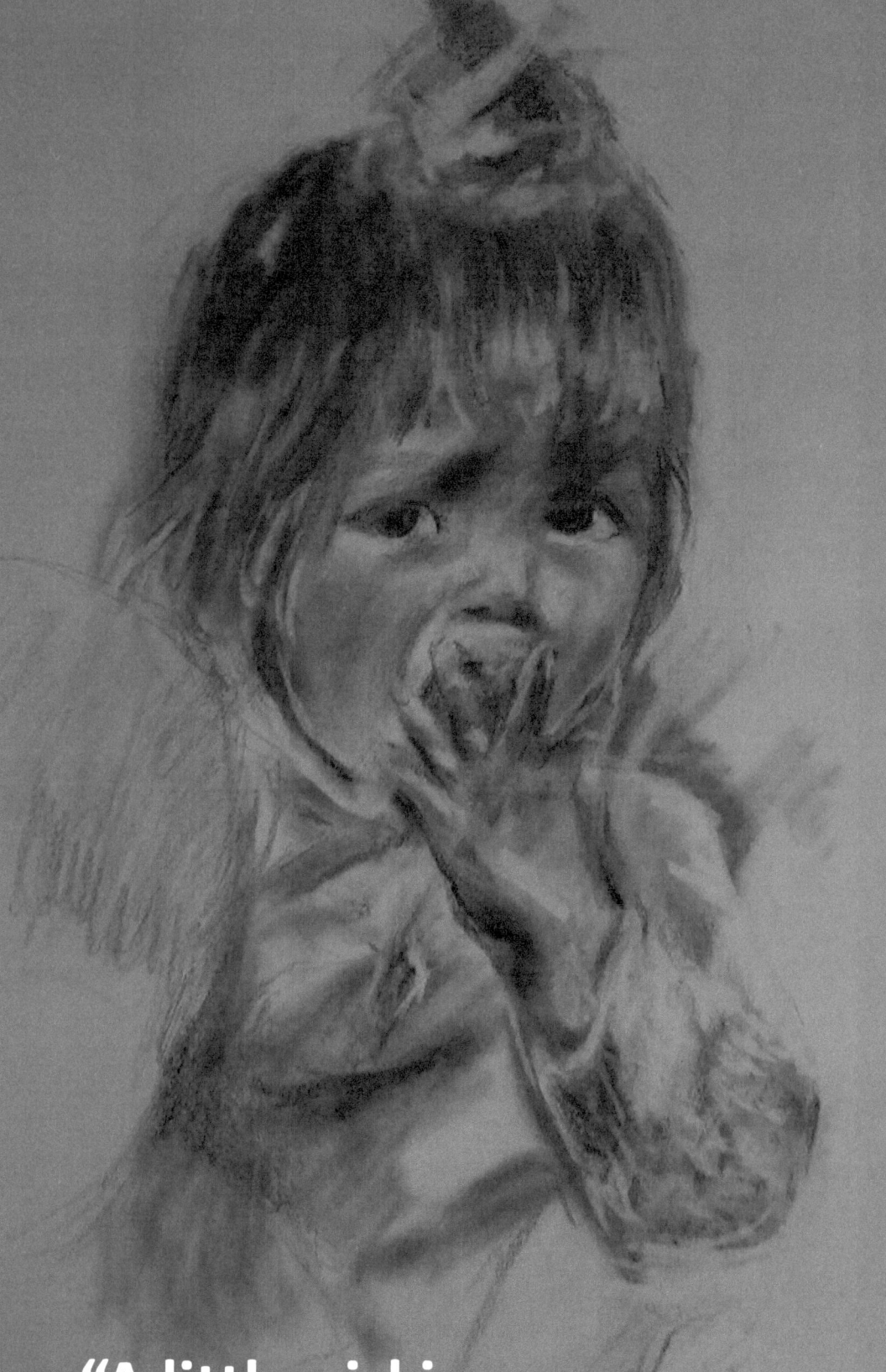

"A little girl is a yawn wrapped in the warmth of sunshine."
- Anonymous

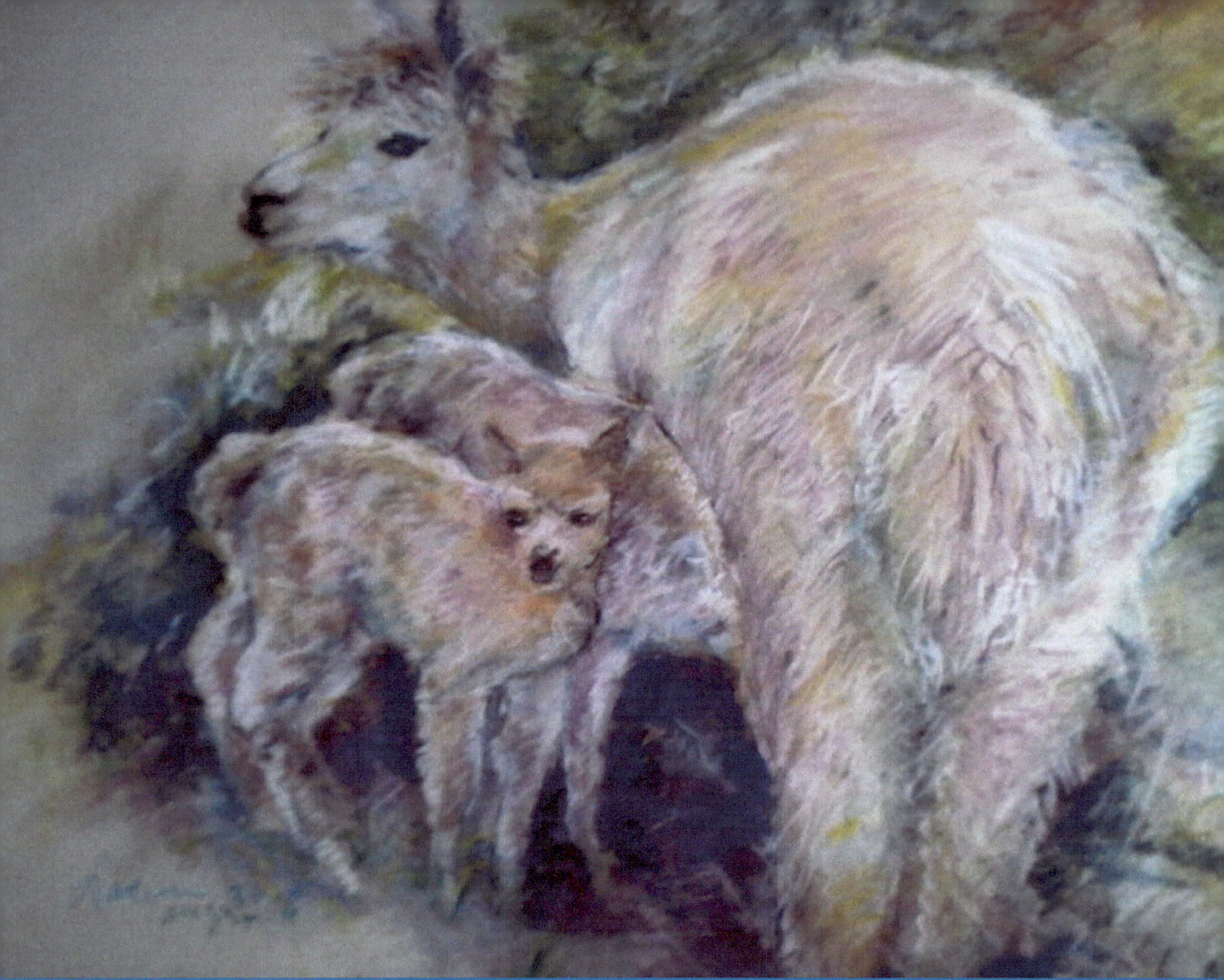

"Spring adds new life and new beauty to all that is."
- Anonymous

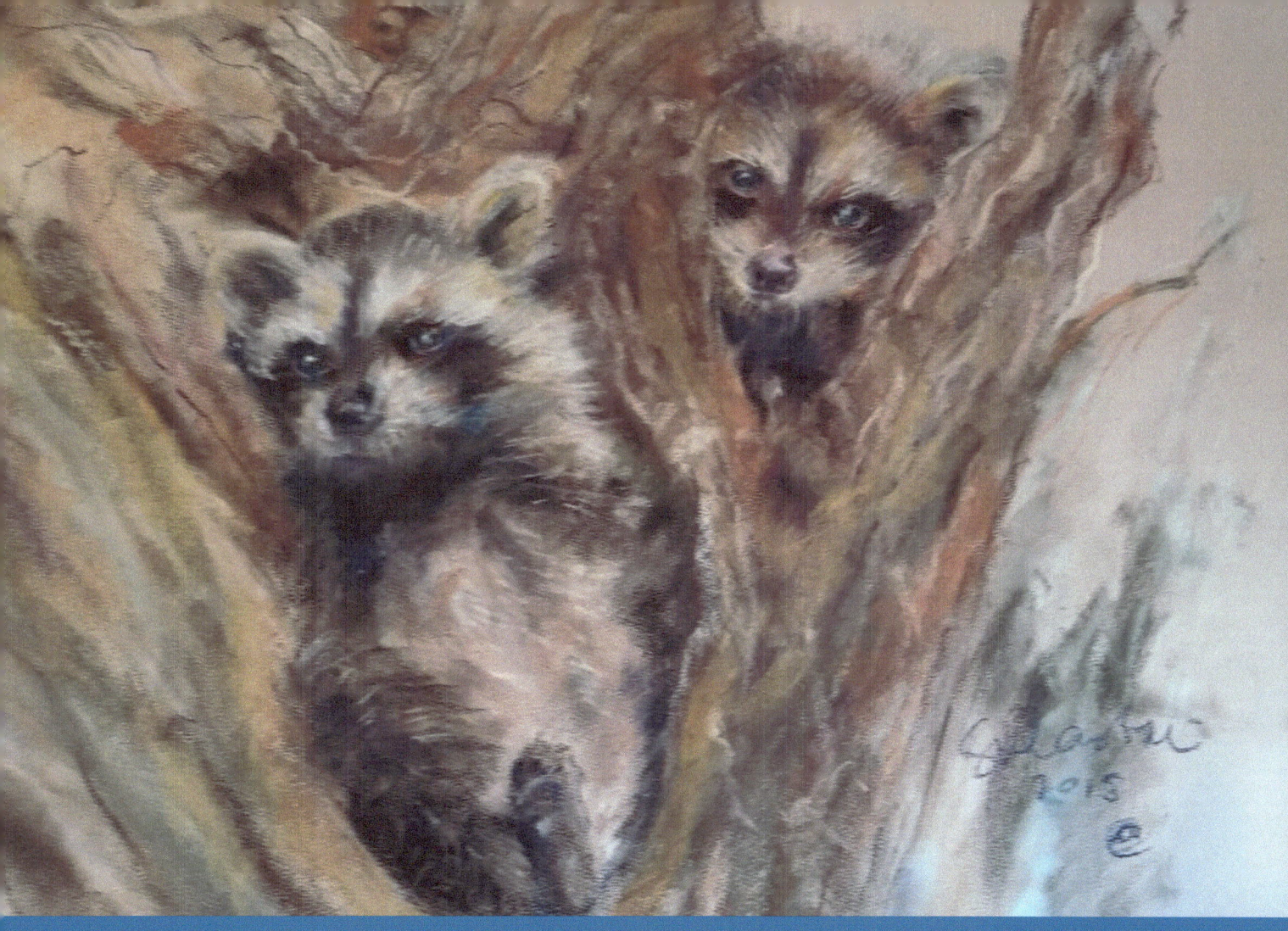

"Why is love easy?
I don't know. And
the raccoons don't
say."
- Robert Fulghum

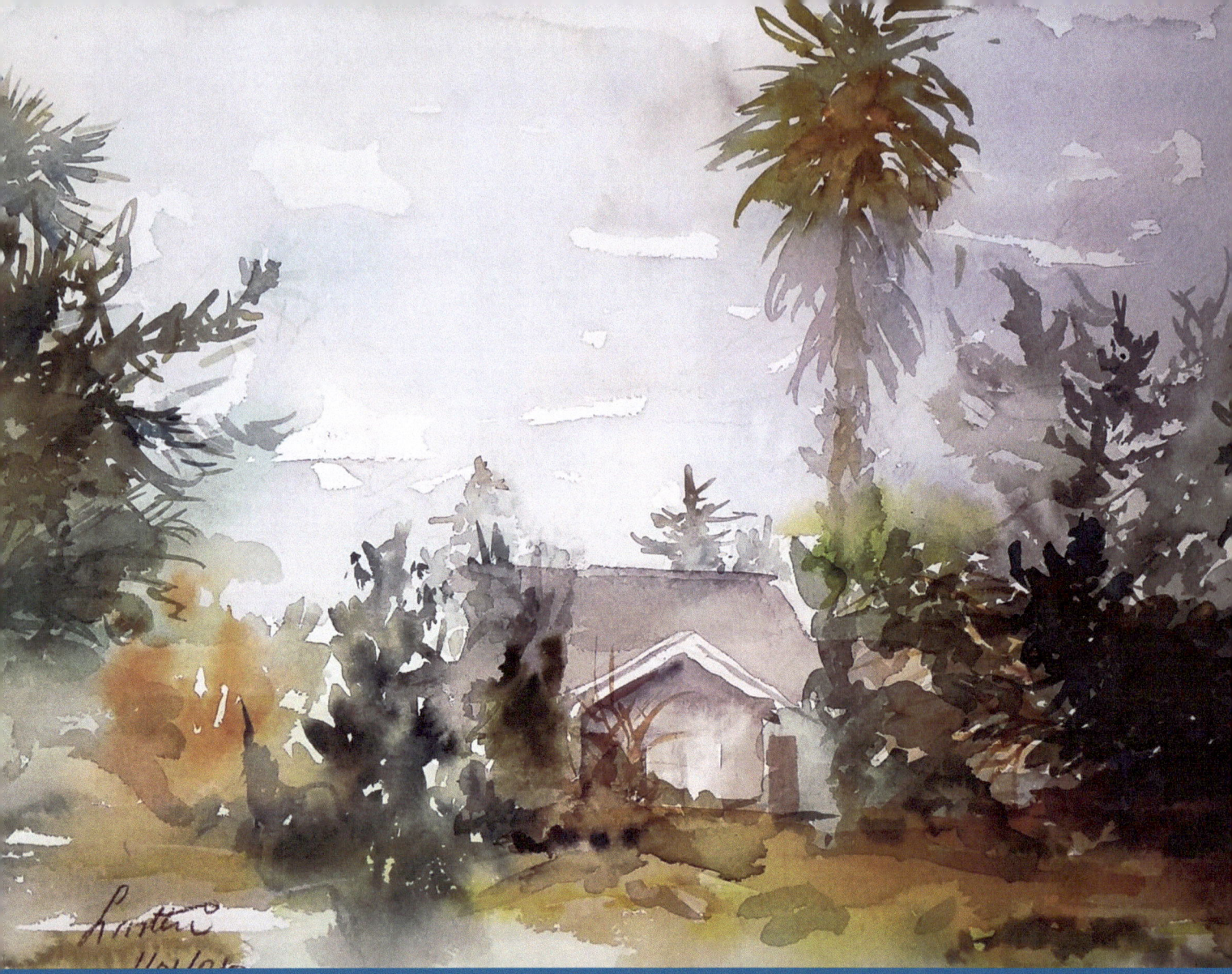

"It's nice when I have days off to go home and relax and literally take the weight off my shoulders and enjoy the simple things."
- Seth Rollins

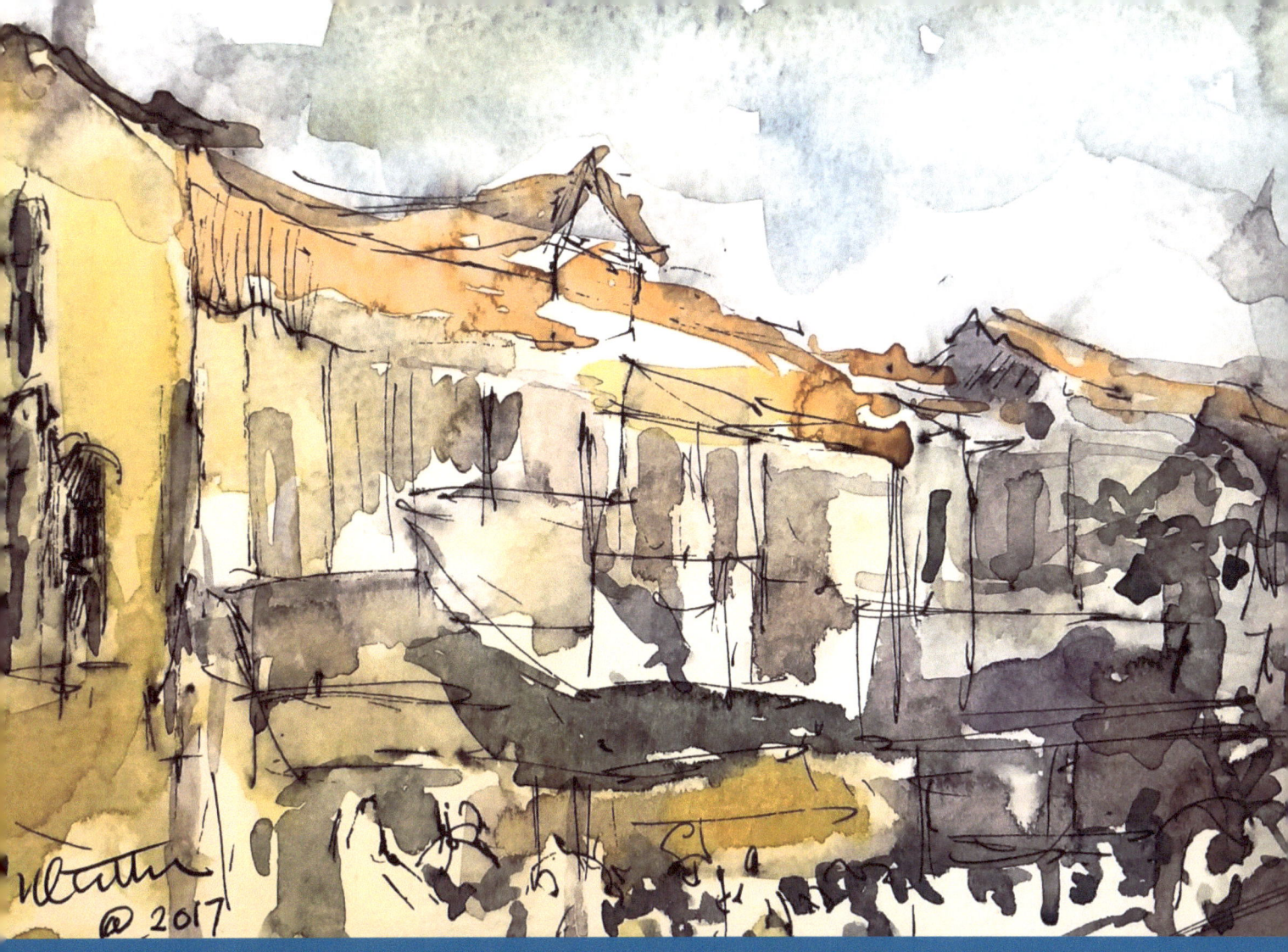

"Living in a small town, one of the keys to survival was your imagination."
- Nick Nolte

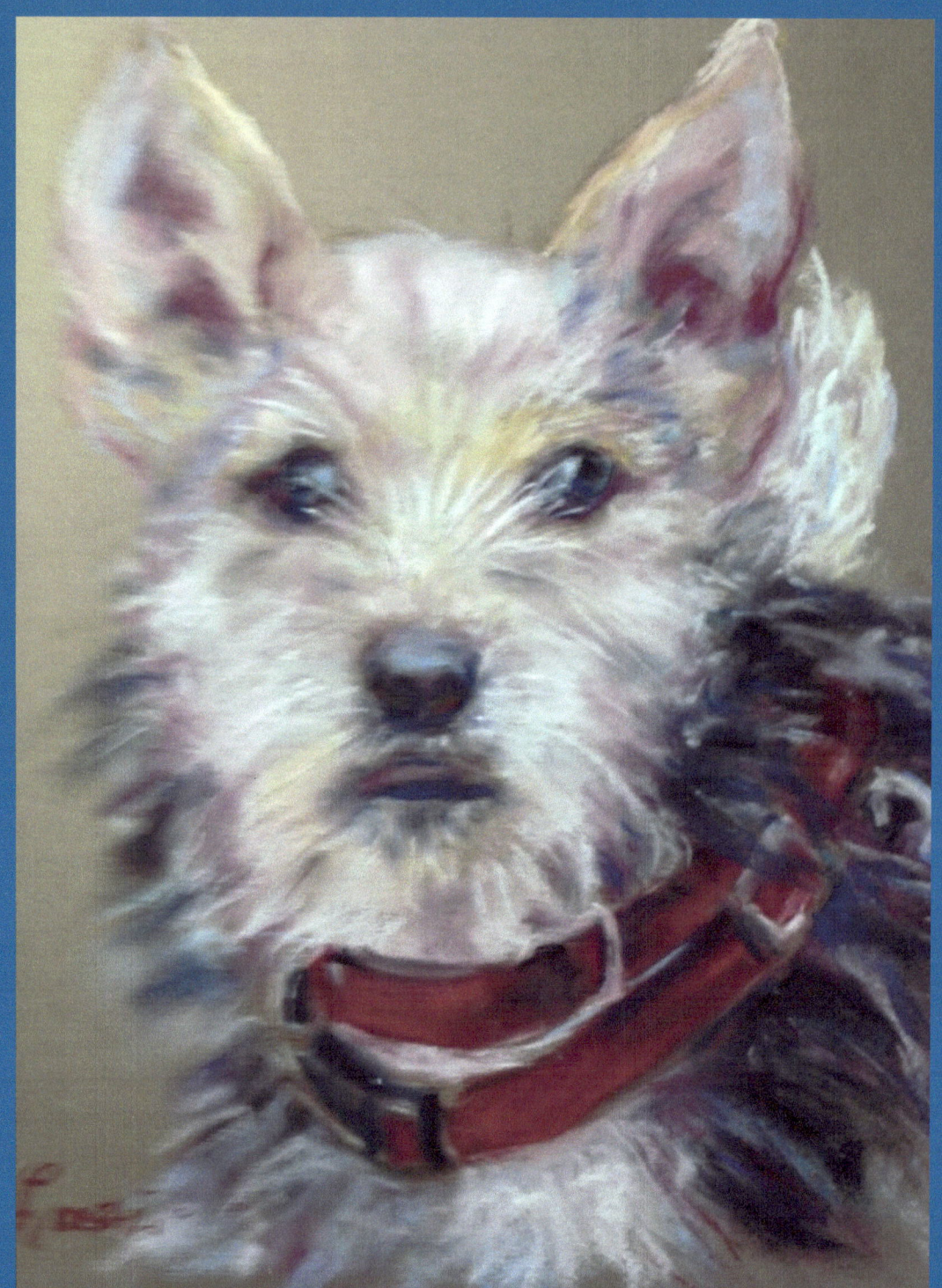

"Handle every stressful situation like a dog. If you can't eat or play with it, just pee on it and walk away." - Anonymous

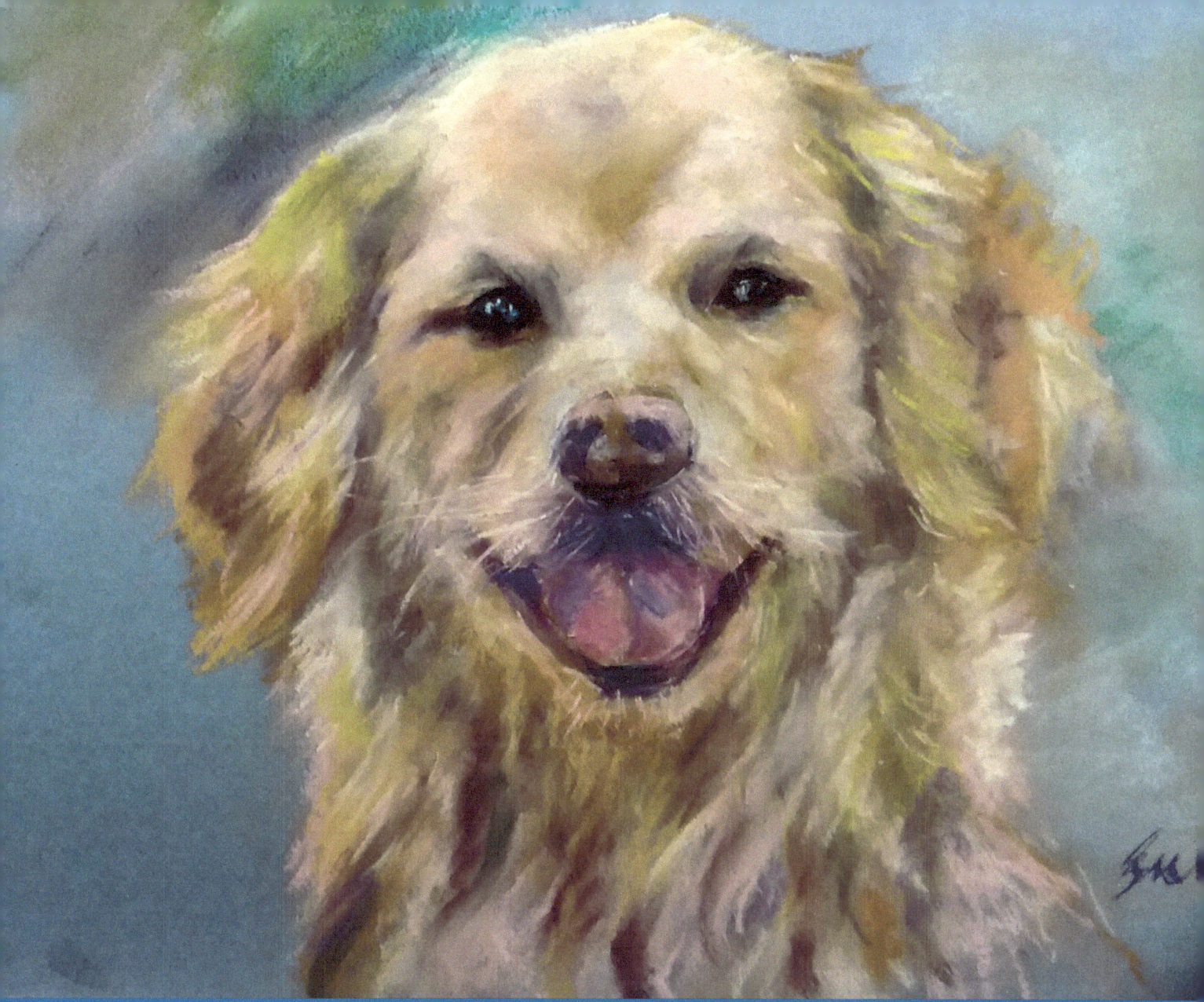

"The best therapist
has fur and four legs."
- Anonymous

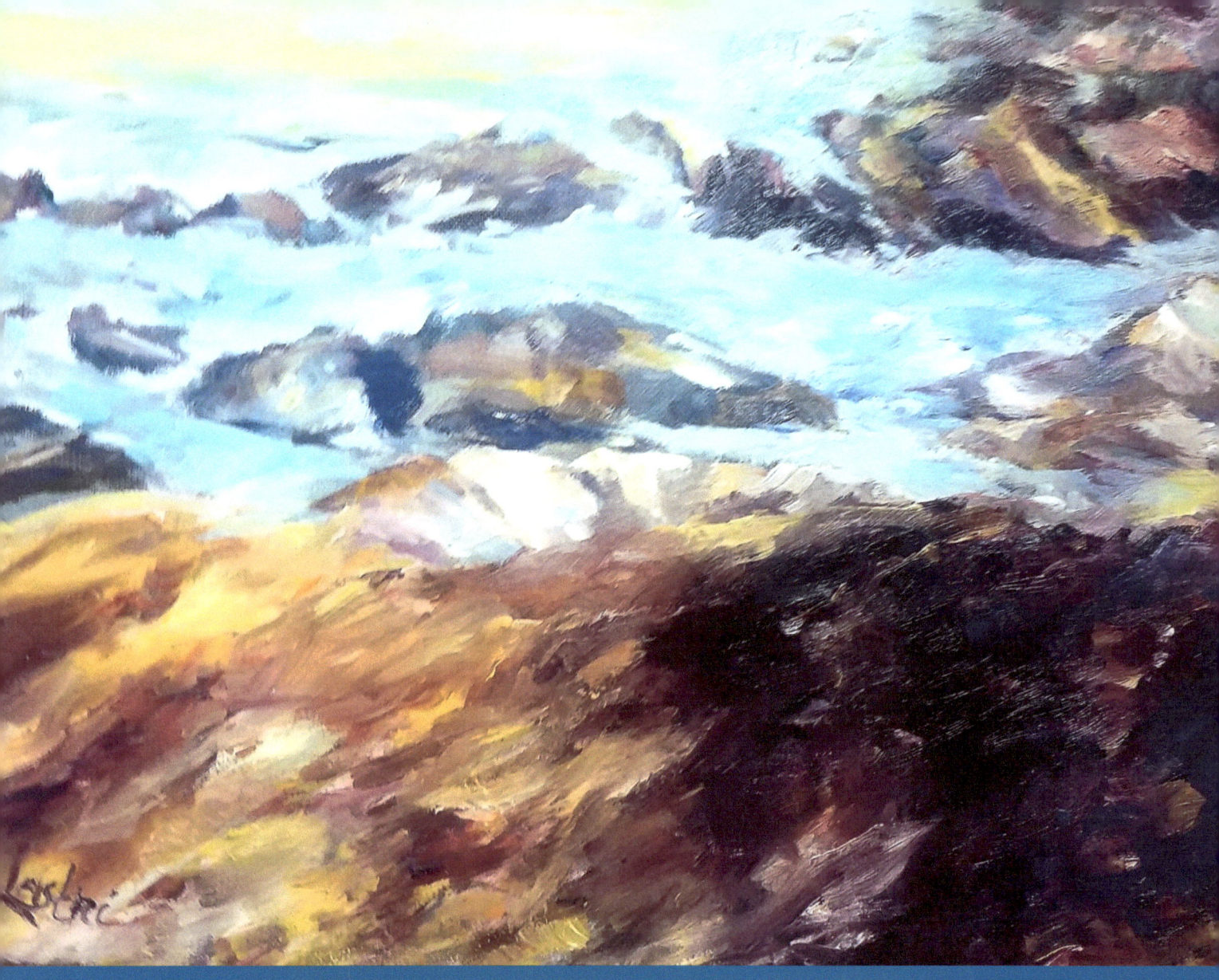

"We are tied to the ocean. And when we go back to the sea, whether it is to sail or to watch, we are going back from whence we came."
- John F. Kennedy

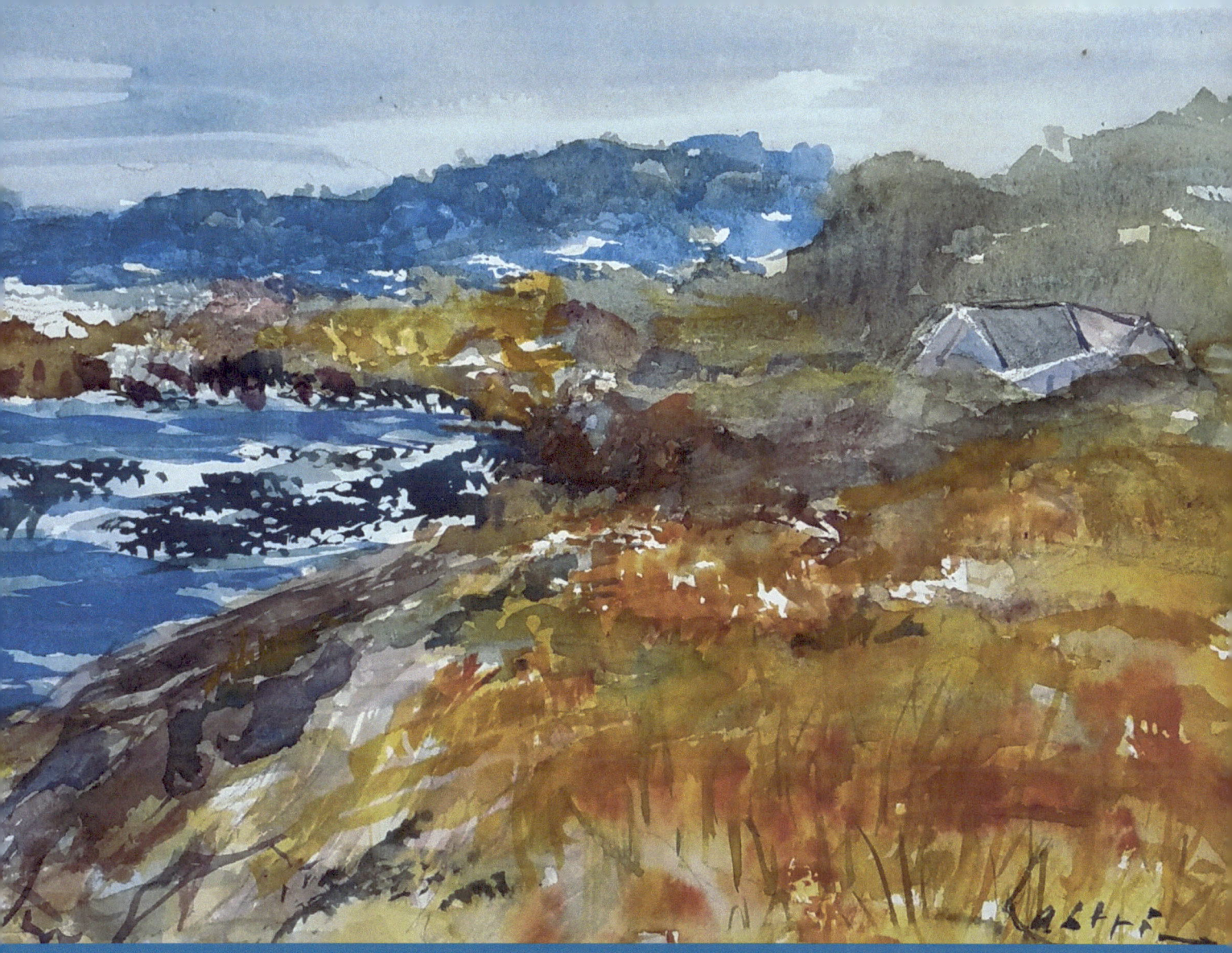

"They say you are closer to heaven in a house by the sea."
- Anonymous

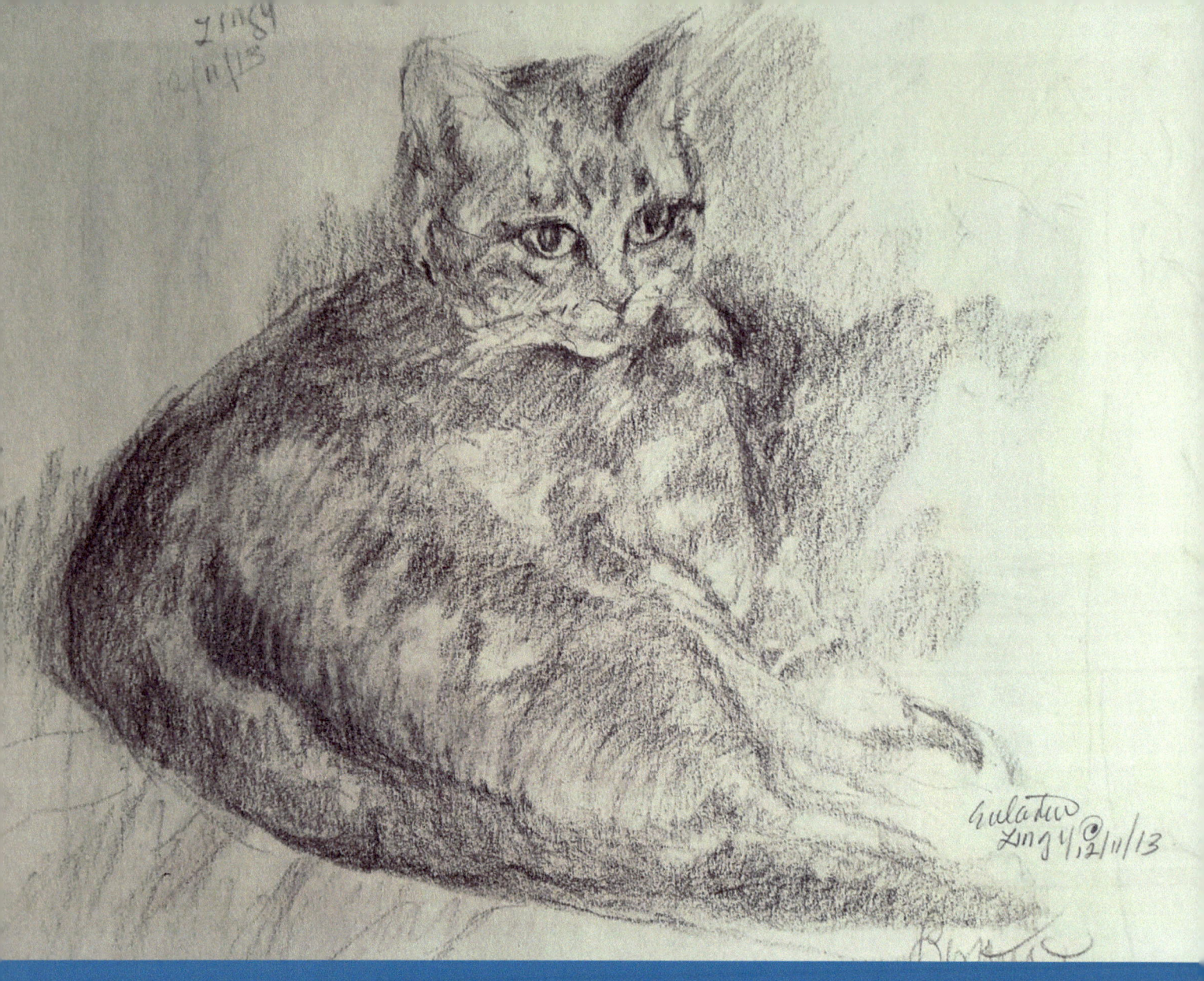

"Time spent with cats is never wasted."
- Sigmund Freud

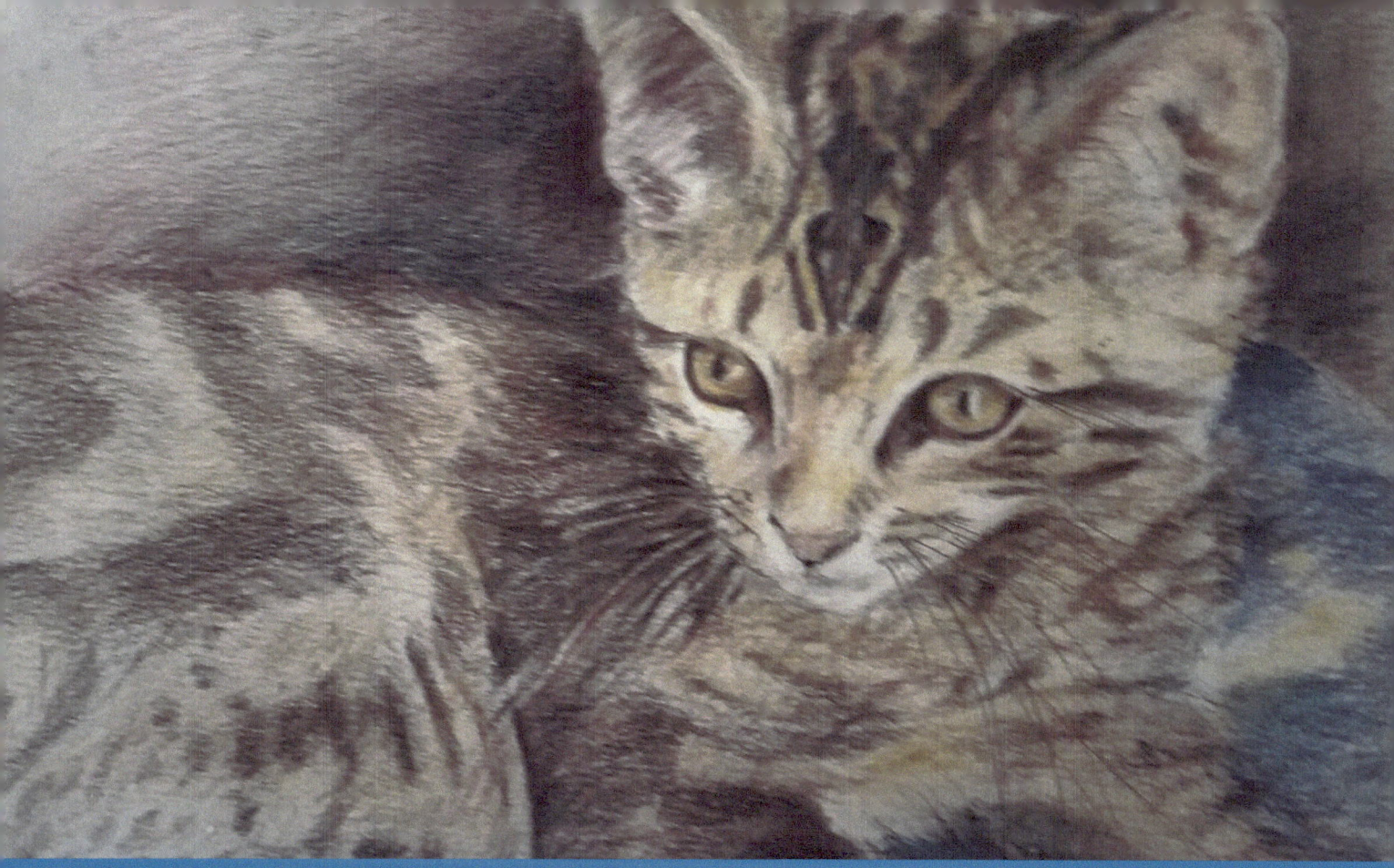

Perhaps one reason we are fascinated by cats is because such a small animal can contain so much independence, dignity, and freedom of spirit. Unlike the dog, the cat's personality is never bet on a human's. He demands acceptance on his own terms.
- Lloyd Alexander

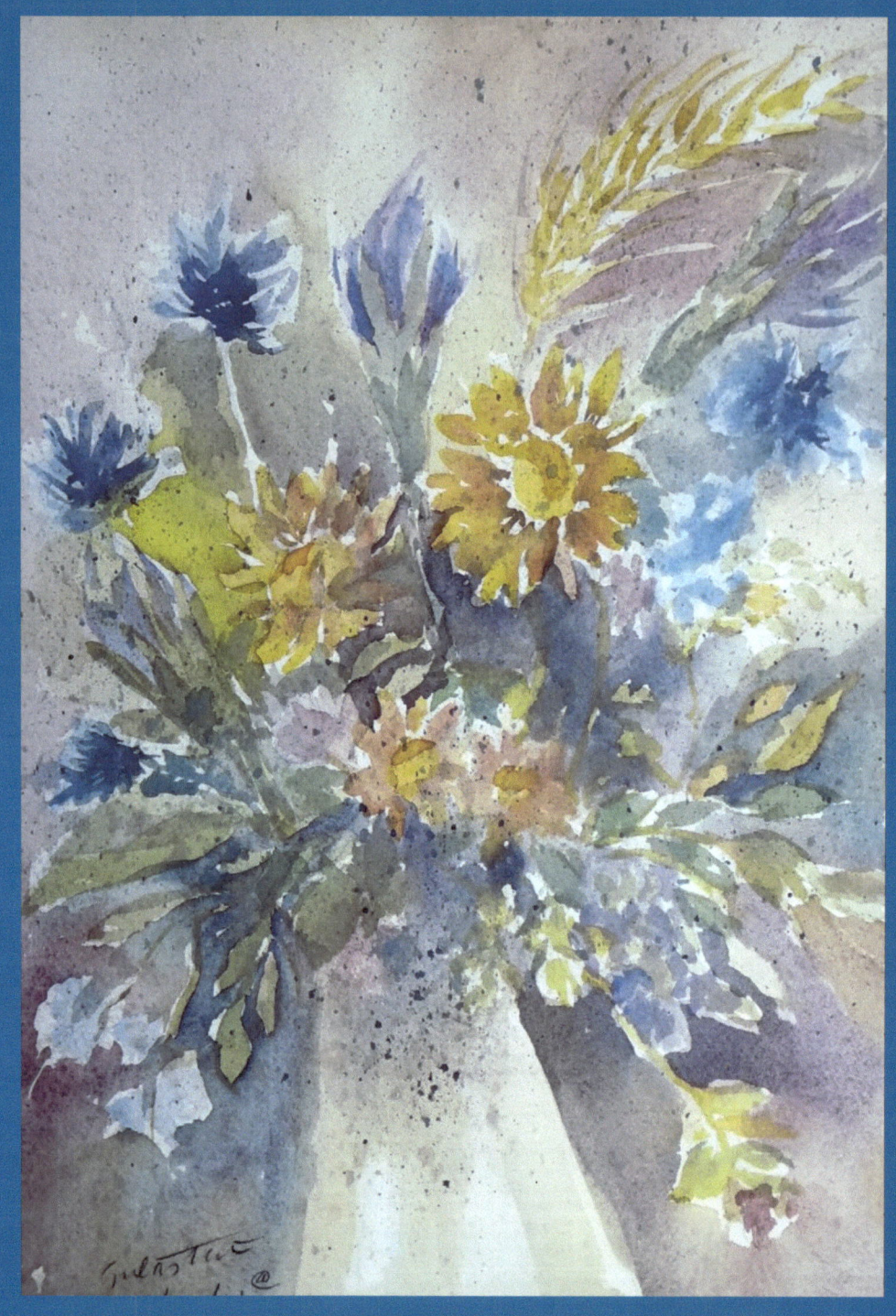

"When I judge art, I take my painting and put it next to a God made object like a tree or flower. If it clashes, it is not art." - Paul Cezanne

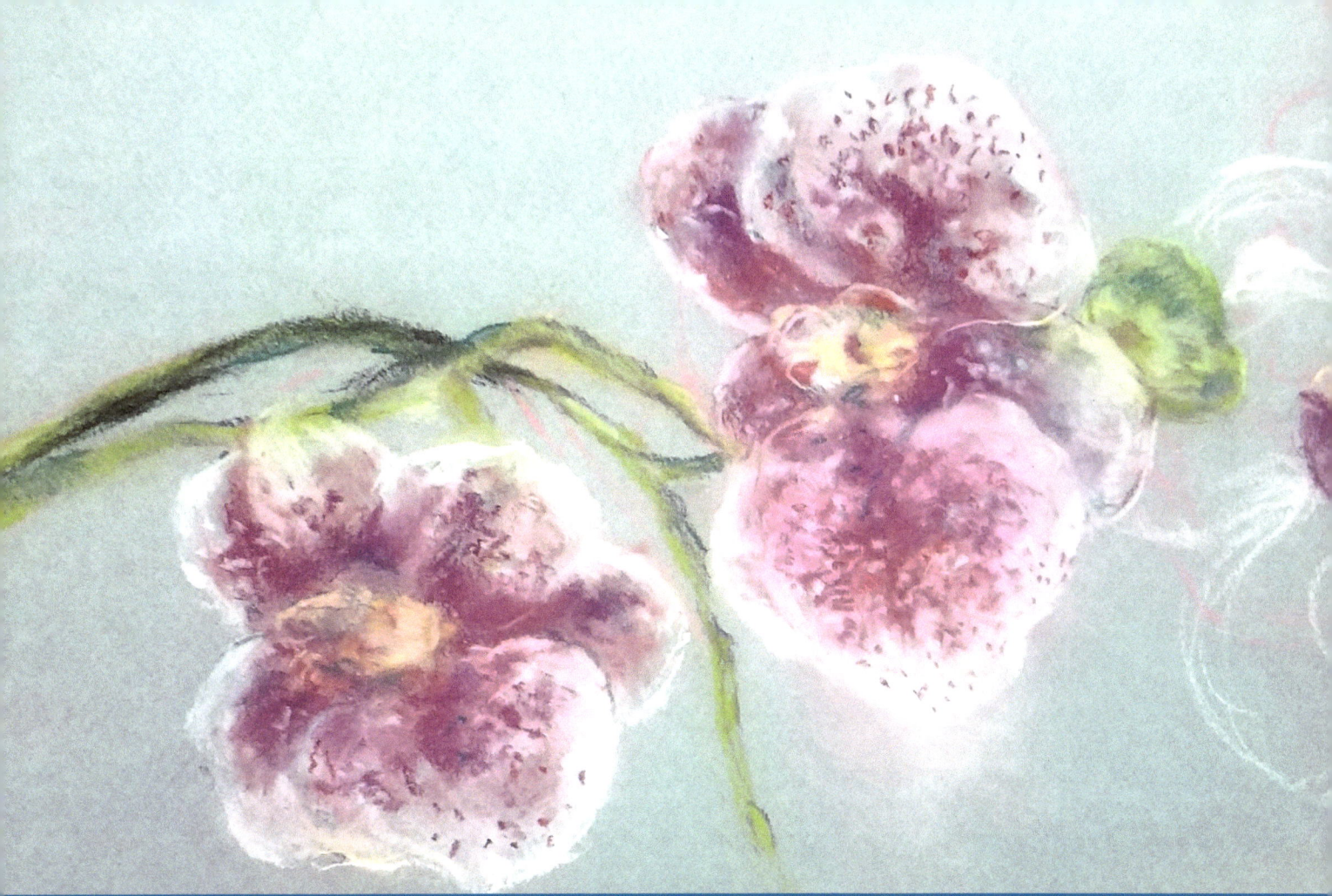

"An orchid in a deep forest
sends out its fragrance
even if no one is around to
appreciate it."
- Confucius

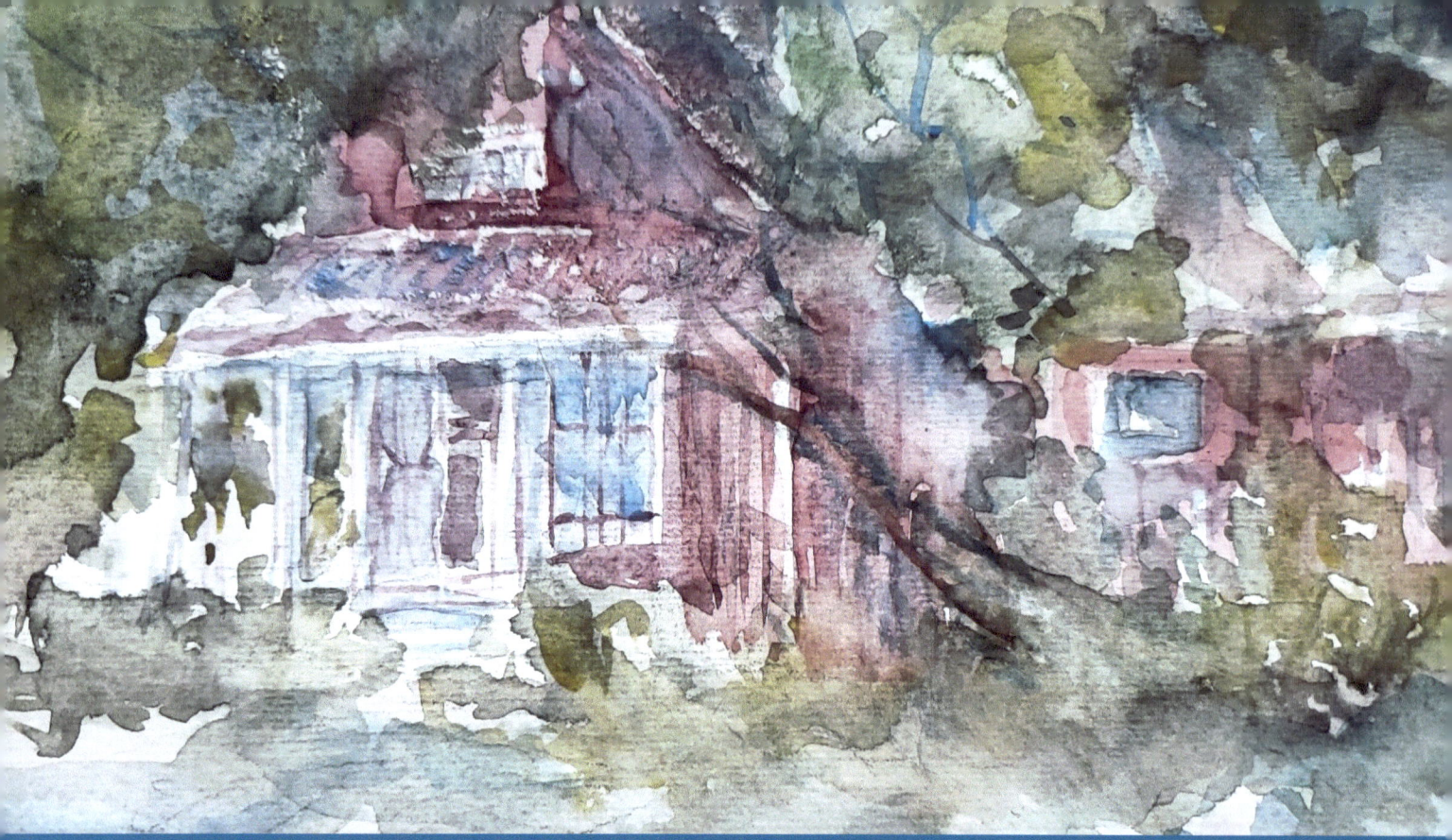

"In a deserted,
empty house
Hidden dreams and
memories
Arouse from a deep
sleep."
- rajesh pramanick

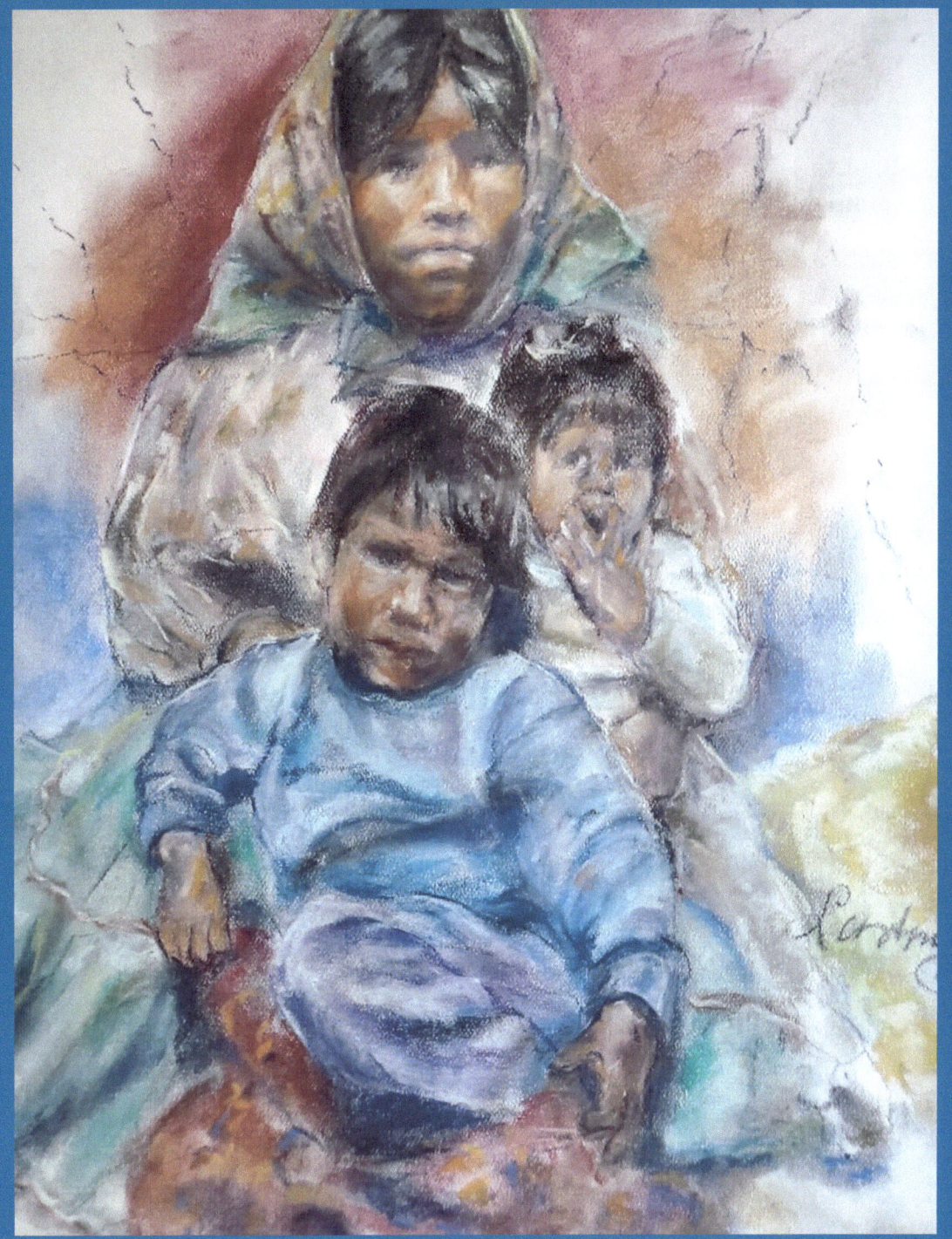

"There are two gifts we should give our children: one is roots and the other is wings." - Anonymous

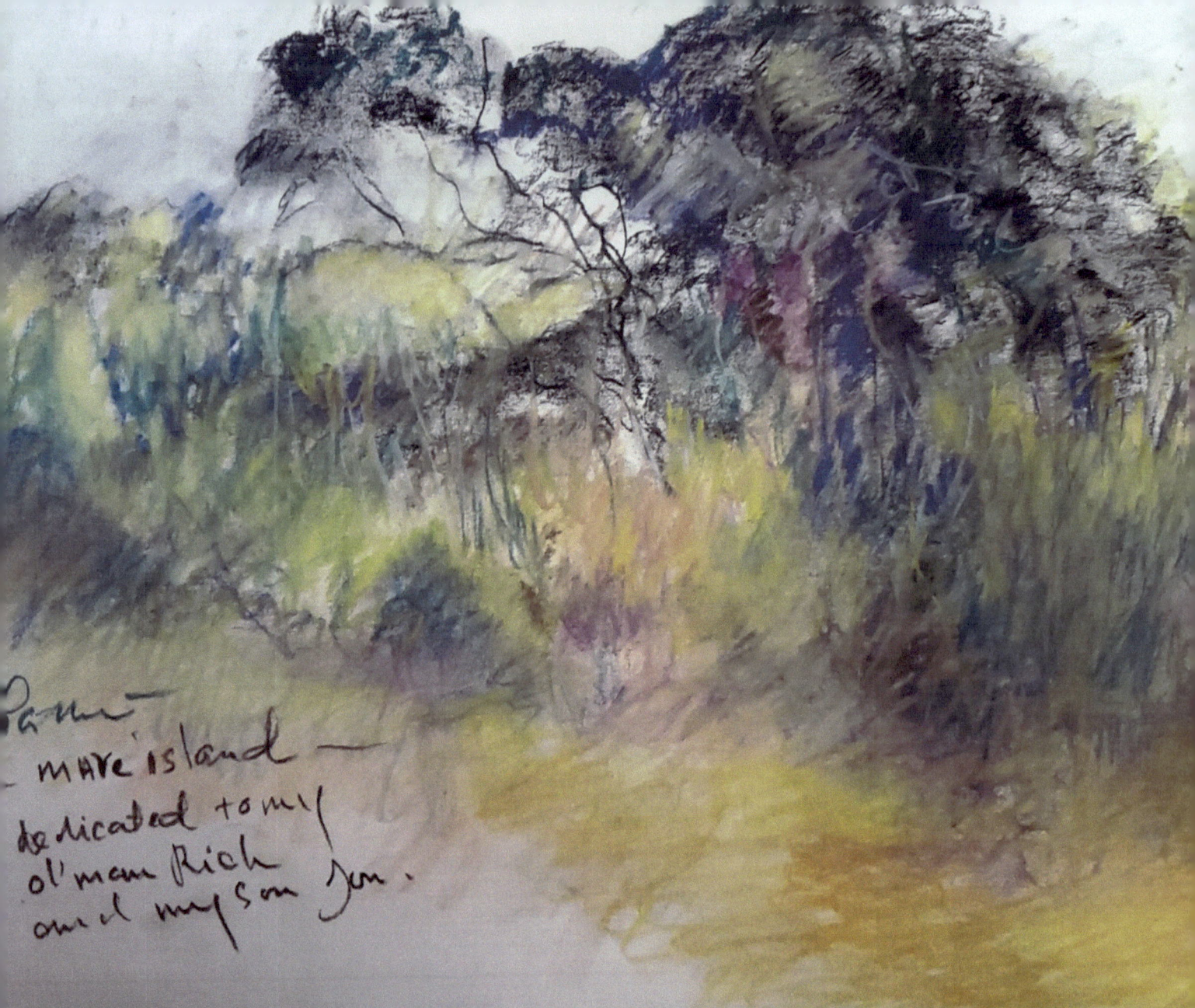

"I like to be grounded by nature, go hiking... go to an isolated island."
- Cote de Pablo

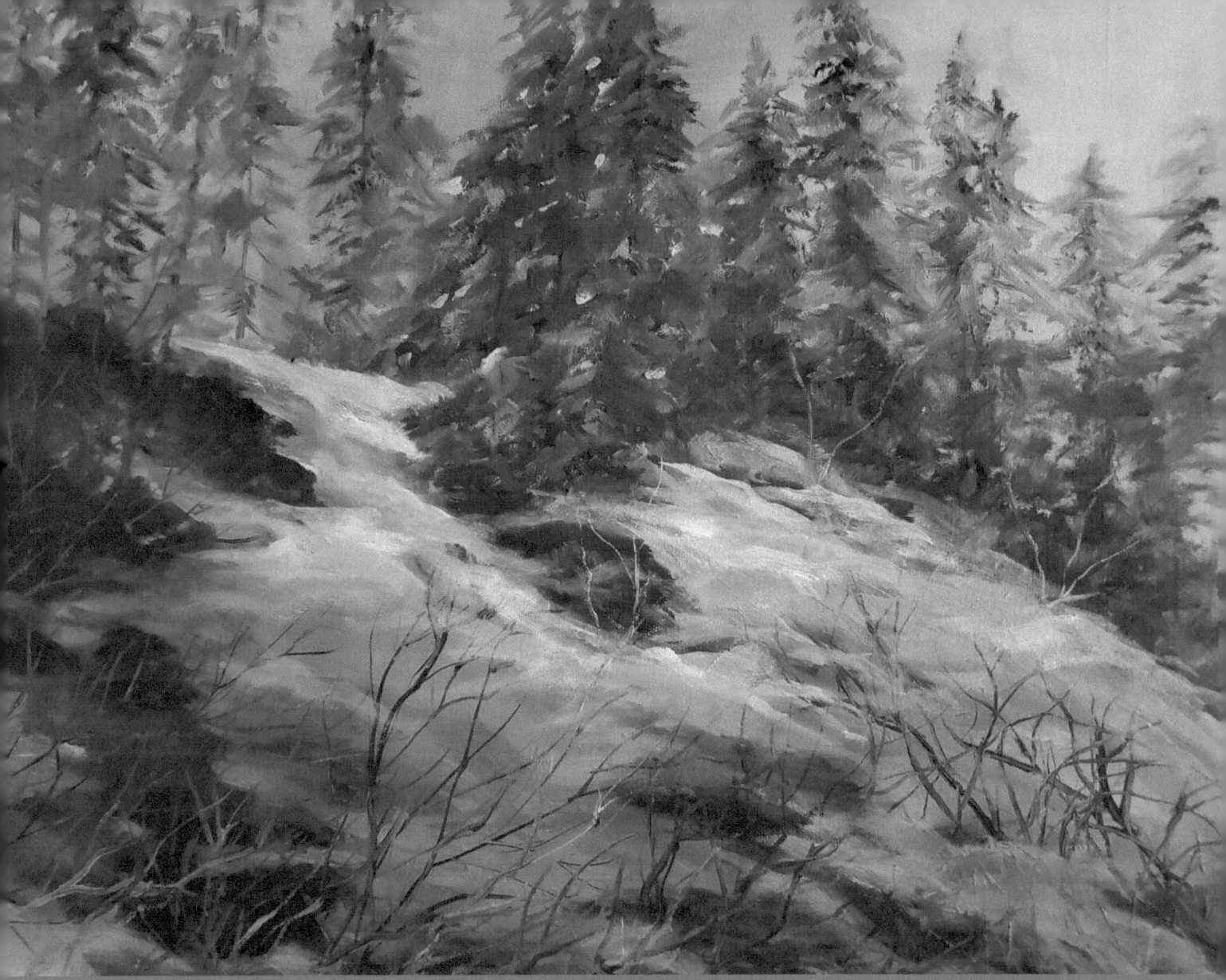

"When your location is a snowy mountain in the winter, the obstacles are pretty extreme."
- Travis Rice

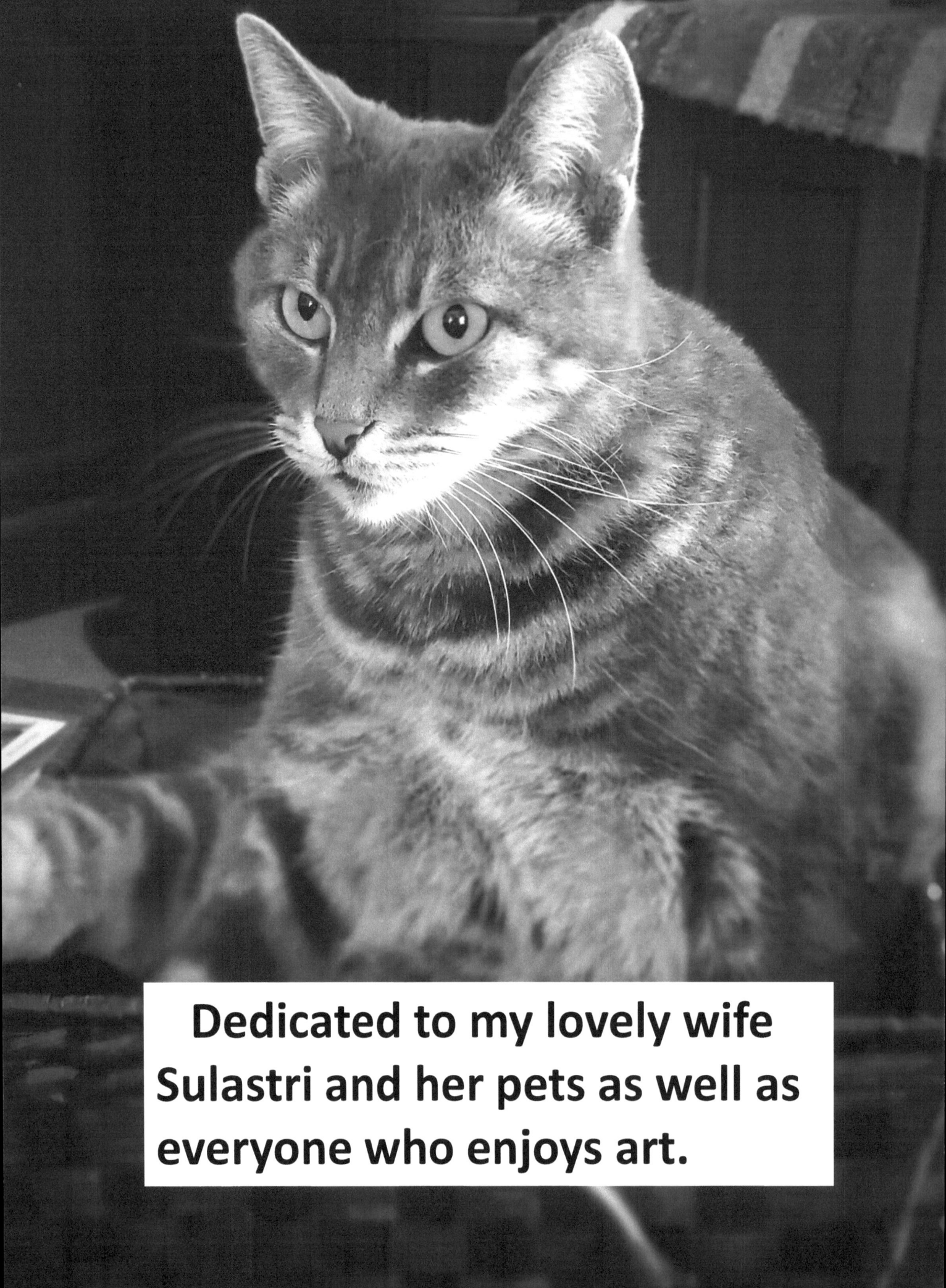

Dedicated to my lovely wife Sulastri and her pets as well as everyone who enjoys art.